Natural Disasters

Quivering Quakes

Julie Richards

Chelsea House Publishers
1974 Sproul Road, Suite 400
Broomall, PA 19008-0914

The Chelsea House world wide web address is www.chelseahouse.com

Library of Congress Cataloging-in-Publication Data Applied for.

ISBN 0-7910-6582-0

First published in 2000 by
Macmillan Education Australia Pty Ltd
627 Chapel Street, South Yarra, Australia, 3141

Copyright © Julie Richards 2001

Edited by Sally Woollett
Text design by Polar Design Pty Ltd
Cover design by Polar Design Pty Ltd
Illustrations and maps by Pat Kermode, Purple Rabbit Productions
Printed in Hong Kong

Acknowledgements
The author and the publisher are grateful to the following for permission to reproduce copyright material:

Cover photograph: Collapsed freeway after earthquake, courtesy of Australian Picture Library/UPPA LTD.

AFP/AAP, p. 16 (bottom); AP/AAP, pp. 16 (top), 18, 21, 24, 26–27; Australian Picture Library/CORBIS, pp. 5 (right), 7, 8 (bottom), 9, 10, 25, 28, 29; Australian Picture Library/Reuters/Bettmann, p. 19; Australian Picture Library/UPPA LTD., p. 15; News Ltd., p. 27 (right); G.R. 'Dick' Roberts Photo Library (NZ), pp. 2–4, 12, 31, 32; PhotoEssentials, p. 23 (bottom); Photolibrary.com, pp. 5 (left), 22, 23 (top).

While every care has been taken to trace and acknowledge copyright the publishers tender their apologies for any accidental infringement where copyright has proved untraceable. Where the attempt has been unsuccessful, the publisher welcomes information that would redress the situation.

Contents

The restless Earth 4

What is an earthquake? 5

What is the Earth made of? 6

How does the Earth move? 8

Where do earthquakes happen? 11

How does an earthquake start? 12

What happens during an earthquake? 13

What kinds of damage can an earthquake do? 15

Measuring earthquakes 19

Can earthquakes be predicted? 21

Protection from earthquakes 24

After an earthquake 28

Record-breaking earthquakes 30

Glossary 31

Index 32

The restless Earth

The Earth is a very restless planet. Even deep beneath the surface, the inside of the Earth is always **moving** and **changing**.

Enormous **pressure** and extremely **high temperatures** build up between the layers of rock that make up our planet.

When this happens, the layers begin to **move**.

Usually, you do not feel this movement because it happens so far beneath you.

However, if you hear a rumbling sound that gets **louder** and **louder**, and if everything around you begins to **sway** and **shake**, an earthquake might just be starting!

EARTHQUAKES

are a natural part of the Earth. However, as our cities grow bigger, and as more people are packed tightly into tall buildings, the risk of death and injury during an earthquake becomes greater. Earthquakes become natural disasters when they threaten people and severely interrupt their daily lives.

What is an earthquake?

An earthquake is when the Earth trembles or vibrates. Sometimes, this trembling can make cracks appear on the Earth's surface. If the movement is strong enough, buildings can fall down and roads can sink, railway tracks can bend, dams can burst and pipes that carry gas can split open, starting fires.

It can take less than a minute for an earthquake to destroy everything.

People rescue their belongings from their collapsed homes in San Francisco, USA after the Loma Prieta earthquake in 1989.

What is the Earth made of?

What do you think the Earth is made of? If it were possible to look inside the Earth, you would see that it is made up of different layers, like an onion that has been sliced in half.

Crust

The thin surface of the Earth is called the **crust**. When you are standing on land, the crust stretches 70 kilometers (44 miles) from your feet towards the center of the Earth beneath you. Under the ocean, the crust is only six kilometers (three miles) thick.

Mantle

The next layer is called the **mantle**. This is where things begin to get hot. Here, the heat has made some of the rocks melt. They turn into a thick, gooey mixture called **magma**.

GUESS WHAT?

The distance from the surface to the Earth's core is about 6,370 kilometers (3,955 miles). It would take about two months to reach the center of the Earth if you were able to walk there!

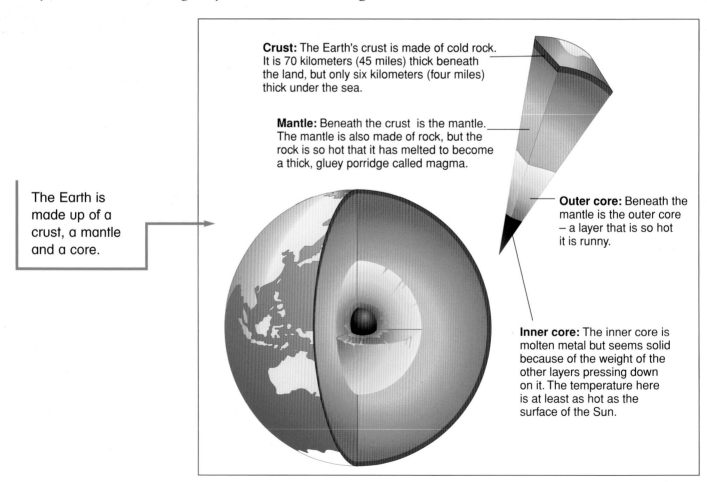

Crust: The Earth's crust is made of cold rock. It is 70 kilometers (45 miles) thick beneath the land, but only six kilometers (four miles) thick under the sea.

Mantle: Beneath the crust is the mantle. The mantle is also made of rock, but the rock is so hot that it has melted to become a thick, gluey porridge called magma.

The Earth is made up of a crust, a mantle and a core.

Outer core: Beneath the mantle is the outer core – a layer that is so hot it is runny.

Inner core: The inner core is molten metal but seems solid because of the weight of the other layers pressing down on it. The temperature here is at least as hot as the surface of the Sun.

Core

The center of the Earth is called the **core**. It has two layers: the outer core and the inner core. The core is made of metal. The outer core is so hot that the metal is runny. The inner core is even hotter, yet it is solid. Why? The other layers press down on the inner core. The weight of all these layers squashes it so tightly into one big lump that it cannot leak out anywhere!

All of this hot magma and metal makes the temperature inside the Earth very high. The Earth's core is prevented from overheating by the escape of hot magma bubbles to the surface. When the magma pushes its way through holes and cracks in the crust, it cools to become solid rock. This is one way new land is made.

Even as you read this book, it is quite likely that new land is being formed somewhere in the world—even under the sea.

New land can be formed under water.

GUESS WHAT?

The temperature of the Earth's core is the same as the surface of the Sun—at least 3,700 degrees Celsius (6,700 degrees Fahrenheit).

How does the Earth move?

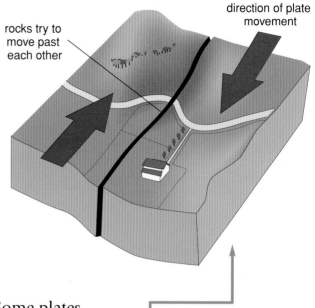

rocks try to move past each other

direction of plate movement

Tectonic plates

The crust does not cover the Earth in one piece like the skin of an orange. Instead, it is divided up into pieces called **tectonic plates**. If you took away the oceans, the Earth's surface would look a bit like a giant jigsaw puzzle.

The Earth's plates do not fit tightly together. Some plates overlap, while others have gaps between them. All the plates float on the magma that flows through the mantle in the same way a boat floats on water. The plates are always moving. It takes thousands of years for the plates to travel any great distance because they are carrying huge oceans and continents on their backs. This movement is known as **continental drift**.

As the magma flows through the mantle, it pushes up against the plates, making them bump and scrape together.

Sometimes two of the Earth's plates bump into each other.

Bending rocks

The rocks in the Earth's tectonic plates have formed over millions of years. You can see the different layers of rock if you look at a cliff like the one in the photograph shown here. What do you notice about the layers?

Disaster Detective

You might like to find out where some of the Earth's continents have travelled in the past. Here is a clue: on a map, look closely at the shapes of Africa and South America.

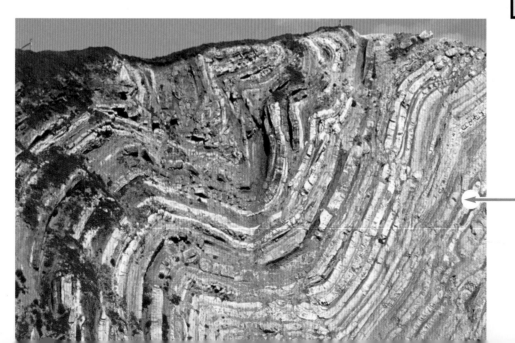

It took incredible strength to bend this rock into waves.

The layers curve like a wave. These rocks were squeezed and bent into this shape over a very, very long time. It would have taken an incredibly powerful force to do this, a force strong enough to make the ground move. A bend in the rock is called a **fold**.

These rocks were most likely squeezed together when two plates bumped into one another on their journey across the world.

Making mountains

When two plates crash together, they can ripple and bend upward into gigantic folds to become mountains. When the plate dragging India crashed into the plate carrying Asia, they folded upwards to make the Himalayan mountains. These two plates are still pushing against one another. This means that, even today, the Himalayas are still growing taller!

TRY THIS

1 Place a piece of paper on a flat surface.

2 With your fingers, press firmly on the paper at both ends.

3 What happens when you push in towards the middle from both ends at once? A large fold will rise upwards in the middle of the paper.

The Himalayas are like a seam showing the join between the two pieces of land.

Breaking plates

The plates do not always bend or fold. Sometimes they just break. If you have ever been unlucky enough to break an arm or a leg, you will know that both pieces of the bone must be held firmly together until they join again. The doctor does this by setting the broken bone in a plaster cast.

When layers of rock are broken they cannot be mended. The break is called a **fault line.** A fault line is a sign of the great pressure the rock layers are under and there will always be a weak spot in that part of the Earth's crust.

Disaster Detective

Did you know that people once believed that earthquakes were caused by the weather? The ancient Greek philosopher Aristotle suggested that winds trapped in deep underground caves might be strong enough to break through the Earth's surface. There are lots of strange and funny stories that have been used to explain earthquakes. Collect some for yourself and compare them.

The San Andreas Fault. A lot of earthquakes happen along this fault line.

How else does the Earth move?

➤ When one plate slides over the top of another, it forces it to sink down into the hot mantle where it begins to melt into magma. This makes the rock around it vibrate.

➤ The water in large dams and **reservoirs** is extremely heavy. This can increase the pressure on the rock layers underneath.

➤ As magma rises up beneath a volcano it can push even heavy rocks out of the way.

All these movements can make the ground shake. However, it is the movement along the edges of the plates that starts the most destructive and deadliest earthquakes.

Where do earthquakes happen?

About one million earthquakes happen around the world each year—that is roughly two a day! Between 40,000 and 50,000 of these earthquakes are felt. The rest are too small or too deep inside the Earth to be noticed by people on the surface. Luckily, only about 40 of these earthquakes are strong enough to cause damage. Although earthquakes can happen at any time and in any part of the world, there are some places where they seem to happen a lot more often than others. Why? Here is a clue: it has something to do with the layers of rock that make up the moving tectonic plates.

Many earthquakes happen along the edges of tectonic plates.

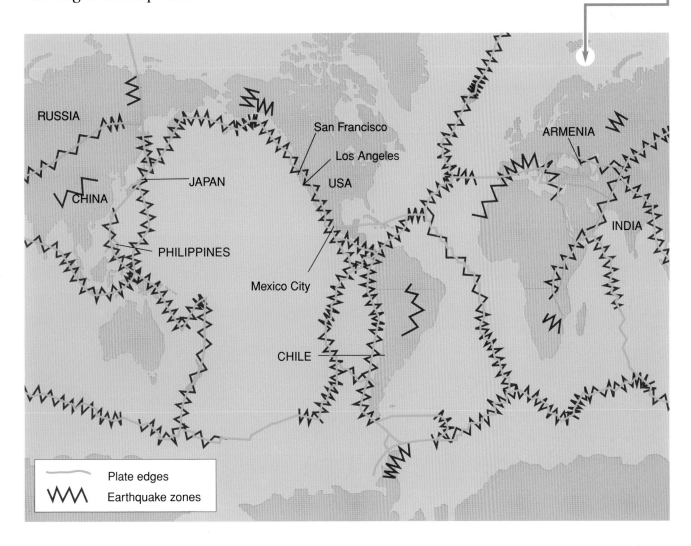

RUSSIA

San Francisco

ARMENIA

Los Angeles

JAPAN

USA

CHINA

INDIA

PHILIPPINES

Mexico City

CHILE

Plate edges

Earthquake zones

How does an earthquake start?

The plates on a fault line rub up and down one another. If the rock is weak it crumbles easily and the plates can grind past. If the rock is strong, the plates keep pushing against each other. Although the plates are jammed together, the powerful forces beneath them keep pushing and pulling in different directions. This stretches the rock and pulls it out of shape.

Eventually, there is so much pressure from this movement that the rock can stretch no further. It snaps back into shape just like a spring. Because the plates move with a sudden jerk, huge amounts of energy are released during this event.

An ancient fault line runs through this cliff at Hawke's Bay, New Zealand.

GUESS WHAT?

An earthquake can release hundreds of times more energy than the nuclear bomb dropped on Hiroshima in Japan in 1945. The energy released by a big earthquake can be the same as setting off millions of tons of explosives at once.

What happens during an earthquake?

Seismic energy

The energy released when rocks snap back into shape during an earthquake is called **seismic energy**. Seismic energy travels through the Earth in waves. If you toss a pebble into a still pond, you can watch the ripples spreading out from the spot where the pebble hit the water. Seismic waves behave in much the same way when they carry the rippling energy of the earthquake.

Not all seismic waves are the same

There are three kinds of seismic waves: P waves, S waves and surface waves.

➤ Primary or P waves are the first waves of the earthquake. They squeeze and release the Earth in much the same way as an accordion is played. P waves are the fastest waves; they make the loud roaring noise that people can hear before the shaking starts.

P waves squeeze and relax the Earth like an accordian.

➤ Shear or S waves arrive after the P wave. They wobble the ground from side to side.

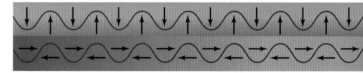
S waves wobble the ground from side to side.

➤ Surface waves move along the ground just like waves on water. They are the slowest, yet most destructive, of all the seismic waves.

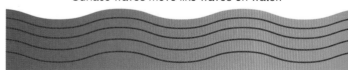
Surface waves move like waves on water.

With all this happening at once, it is no wonder buildings topple and huge cracks appear in the ground.

When surface waves move over the ground it is possible to see them. Many people have reported seeing the ground or road heave itself up into great waves that roll towards them. When this happens it must be like trying to surf! It is easy to see why most people cannot stand up during big earthquakes.

Focus

Even though you can feel the ground vibrating beneath your feet, the earthquake is really happening a long way underground. The spot where the seismic energy is being released is called the **focus**. It can be as far as 600 kilometers (370 miles) below the Earth's surface. However, when the focus of a small earthquake is close to the surface, the shaking is more violent and causes much greater **devastation** than some bigger earthquakes do.

The distance of the focus underground determines the strength of an earthquake on the surface.

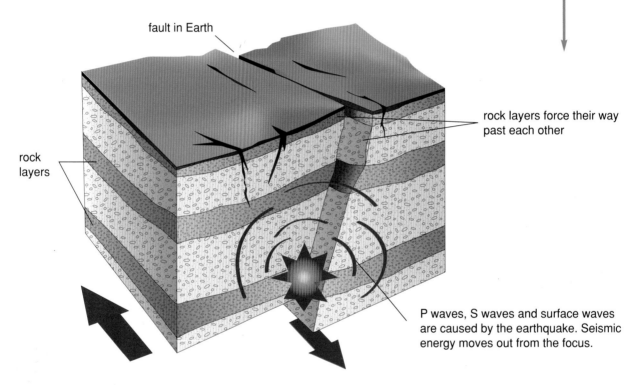

fault in Earth

rock layers

rock layers force their way past each other

P waves, S waves and surface waves are caused by the earthquake. Seismic energy moves out from the focus.

Epicenter

Seismic waves travel through the Earth in all directions. They come up to the surface as well as going deeper into the Earth. The point on the surface where the waves are strongest is always above the spot where the earthquake starts. It is called the **epicenter**.

Usually, the most damage done by the earthquake happens near the epicenter. The seismic waves carry the shaking of the earthquake for hundreds of kilometers. The further they travel the weaker they become, just like the ripples in a pond.

What kinds of damage can an earthquake do?

Earthquakes can cause all kinds of problems. How an earthquake affects people will depend on where it happens and how deep within the Earth its focus is. Even a small earthquake can cause big problems if lots of people happen to live close by. The freeway that collapsed during Japan's Kobe earthquake in 1995 was practically empty. If the earthquake had happened two hours later it would have been jammed with people travelling to work and school. There would have been many more deaths and injuries.

This freeway collapsed during an earthquake in Japan in 1995. A newspaper reporter said he felt like he was riding on a giant rollercoaster.

Liquefaction

The ground is not always as solid as it looks. It might be made up of loosely packed sand and gravel or there might be an underground stream running nearby. An earthquake can force underground water to rise into the sand and gravel, turning it into a liquid. Scientists call this **liquefaction** (pronounced *li kwi fac shun*).

Liquid soil is like **quicksand**. Anything built on it begins to sink because the ground in its changed state cannot take the weight of the buildings.

Earthquakes can loosen even the biggest rocks.

Taiwan is a small island with a large population. Fitting everybody into this tiny space is a problem. Building tall blocks of flats is one way of making sure that everybody has a home. Unfortunately, many of these buildings are not very safe during earthquakes.

Landslides, avalanches and rock falls

Earthquakes usually only last a few seconds. Their sudden jerky movement can shake rocks, soil and snow from mountainsides. When this happens, landslides, **avalanches** and rock falls may thunder down the slopes, flattening forests and crushing any towns and farms below.

Floods

Falling rocks and sliding soil can rush down into rivers and lakes, making them overflow and flood nearby land. Sometimes, the course of the river may be changed when large boulders crash into it and stop the river from flowing. Rocks can pile up and make the river go in a new direction. This is not good if the people living there depend on the river to water their crops or to catch fish.

Dams must be carefully checked for earthquake damage. Because of the weight of the water, even tiny cracks in a dam wall can be disastrous.

GUESS WHAT?

After an earthquake in Chile, tsunamis spread out in all directions and travelled as far as New Zealand and Japan. Even though they had travelled a great distance, the waves were still six meters (20 feet) high when they struck the coast. What caused the earthquake? A 1,000-kilometer (625 mile) slab of the Earth's crust was pushed underneath South America after rock layers in the ocean floor snapped.

Giant ocean waves

Earthquakes can cause floods in another way. Underwater earthquakes disturb the ocean floor. They make the water at the bottom of the ocean surge upwards into a gigantic wave called a **tsunami.**

Tsunamis can kill more people than an earthquake itself. The tsunami travels many hundreds or thousands of kilometers across the ocean and can flood countries a long way away from the epicenter.

If crops and farmland are covered with salt water, thousands of people can die of starvation and disease long after the killer wave has passed. You do not have to be on top of an earthquake to be in danger.

Half a Million Homes Burn in Japan

The Great Kanto earthquake of 1923 struck Tokyo just before lunchtime. In those days, a traditional Japanese lunch was cooked on a small, charcoal brazier—something similar to an indoor barbecue.

Many of these braziers had been lit only minutes before the earthquake was felt. As the shockwaves toppled houses, the braziers overturned, starting fires that raged through much of Tokyo. Most of the 143,000 people that died in the earthquake were killed by the fire.

Fire

Perhaps one of the most frightening things that can happen during an earthquake is fire. Pipes that carry gas can twist and break, spilling the invisible gas into the air. If there are sparking power lines, explosion and fire can happen before the power supply is shut off. The water pipes may have also burst, leaving no water available to put out the fires.

Aftershocks

The plates that have moved will settle down and join together again. As they do so, smaller, trembling movements may be felt. These little earthquakes are called **aftershocks**. Although they are much smaller than the earthquake, aftershocks can still shake damaged buildings enough to make them collapse.

Gas leaks are very dangerous because the gas is invisible. These two policemen are wearing gas-proof outfits.

Measuring earthquakes

Seismographs

The scientists who find out about earthquakes are called **geologists**. They use a special instrument called a **seismograph** to measure earthquakes.

A seismograph picks up the vibrations made by an earthquake and records them as a wavy line. P waves are the fastest waves sent out by an earthquake and are always the first to be detected by seismographs.

There are seismographs in all parts of the world. They form a special worldwide seismograph network. This helps geologists to work out exactly where an earthquake's epicenter is.

Not only do geologists need to know where and when an earthquake happens, they also want to know how big it is. Geologists use something called the Richter Scale to measure earthquakes.

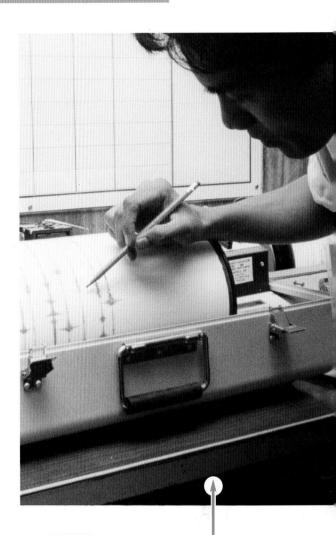

A seismograph is a paper-covered drum that spins under a pen. When the Earth moves or vibrates, the pen makes a wavy line on the paper.

Read All About It!

Famous Chinese Astronomer and Mathematician Invents Seismograph

In 132 AD, Zhang Heng invented the first known seismograph. Made of a shiny metal called bronze, it was shaped like a flower vase and had eight dragon heads hanging upside-down around the top. Inside was a heavy metal ball. The seismograph was placed at the center of a circle of eight bronze frogs. Each frog was directly beneath a dragon head.

When an earthquake happened, the ball would be dropped from a dragon's mouth and into a frog's mouth. Although it could not measure the actual size of the earthquake, it was able to show the direction from which the earthquake was coming.

Richter Scale

The Richter Scale is not the same as the scales that we use to weigh things. The Richter Scale is a special formula that uses numbers to describe the size or **magnitude** of an earthquake. It is named after the scientist who thought of it, Charles Richter. Each number on the Richter Scale represents an earthquake that is ten times more powerful than the number before it. The scale starts at zero and goes as high as necessary. No earthquake has measured more than 10. Earthquakes measuring 5 and above are usually enough to cause damage and death.

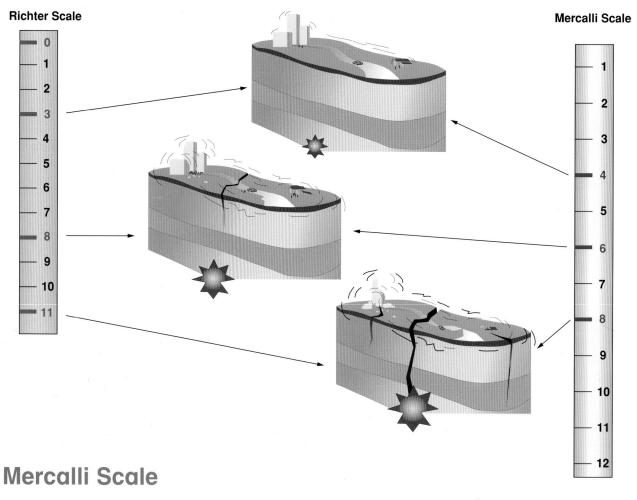

Richter Scale

0
1
2
3
4
5
6
7
8
9
10
11

Mercalli Scale

1
2
3
4
5
6
7
8
9
10
11
12

Comparing the Mercalli and Richter scales.

Mercalli Scale

Earthquakes can also be measured using the Mercalli Scale. The Mercalli Scale does not measure an earthquake in the same way as the Richter Scale. Instead of using mathematics to work out the size of an earthquake, the Mercalli Scale rates an earthquake by describing the damage caused and how much the earthquake has shaken objects. The scale goes from 1 to 12.

Can earthquakes be predicted?

Most people killed or injured in an earthquake are usually struck by falling **debris** or buried alive when buildings collapse. It would be wonderful if geologists could find out when earthquakes were going to happen. Then many people could be moved away to safety before the earthquake started.

Knowing when something is going to happen is called a prediction. Geologists have been trying very hard to find a way to predict earthquakes so that people can be warned, but they have had little success so far.

Haicheng

In 1970, a chain of small **earth tremors** began around Haicheng in northeastern China. Geologists call these small tremors **foreshocks**. Foreshocks are like an early warning system because they sometimes come before an earthquake. By 1975, geologists noticed that water flowing from natural springs had become too muddy to drink. When rats began to gather together and snakes woke early from **hibernation**, the geologists decided that an earthquake must be about to happen. Ninety thousand people were evacuated from Haicheng. Two days later, an earthquake measuring 7.3 on the Richter Scale destroyed nearly every building in the city.

This three-year-old girl was rescued 38 hours after an earthquake in Korfez, Turkey, in 1999.

Earthquake detecting equipment

Geologists study the Earth's movements very carefully. They use complicated instruments that have been specially designed for the type of measuring jobs they must do.

Laser beams

Close to the San Andreas Fault in the United States of America (USA), geologists shine thin beams of special light across the fault. These are laser beams. The laser beams hit the rock on the other side of the fault and are reflected back. Geologists know that laser beams travel at the speed of light, so they can measure the time it takes for the beam to hit its target and return. If it takes longer or shorter than the last time, they will know that the rocks have moved.

You might think that no movement at all is a good thing. However, sometimes a big earthquake comes after the rocks have been still and quiet for a long time. Lots of little movements can help relieve the pressure the rock is under by releasing the seismic energy a little bit at a time.

GUESS WHAT?

The plates on the San Andreas Fault in the USA have been locked together for a long time. Geologists believe that this is where the next big earthquake will happen. There is more earthquake monitoring equipment here than anywhere else in the world.

These laser beams can measure even tiny movements in the San Andreas Fault in the USA.

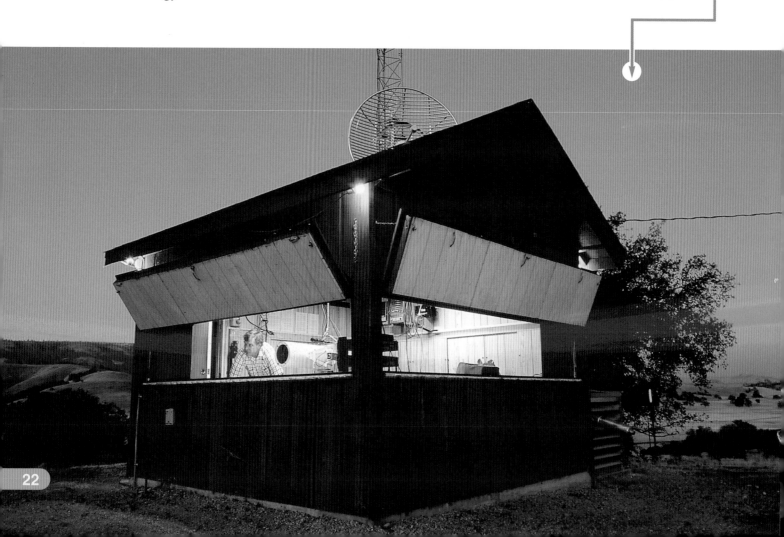

Strainmeter

Earthquakes happen when rocks are under an enormous pressure or strain. Geologists can measure the strain using something called a **strainmeter**. Even though it is possible to measure strain, geologists still do not know just how much strain the rocks can take before they jolt and start an earthquake.

This geologist is checking the instruments used to measure movements in the Earth's rocks.

Tiltmeter

Sometimes, the growing pressure makes the rocks swell or bulge upwards. This can change the way the ground slopes. These changes are so tiny that you cannot see them. Geologists need to use a **tiltmeter** to record them.

Satellites

Geologists also get measurements from space. Satellites spinning around the Earth have instruments that can measure even slight movements in the Earth's plates.

Geologists hope that all this measuring will help them to work out when an earthquake might be about to happen. Unfortunately, predicting how big the earthquake will be is something they cannot do.

Satellites can see a lot from space. They can measure the smallest movements in the Earth's plates.

Protection from earthquakes

Earthquakes cannot be prevented. However, the damage they do can be reduced by earthquake-proofing cities in high-risk areas. Knowing how to evacuate people from a building in a calm and orderly way can help save lives and prevent unnecessary injury. If it is not possible to evacuate, sheltering under strong furniture such as a heavy wooden table or desk can help protect against falling objects.

Planning for disaster

In some countries people are used to living with earthquakes. In Japan, they have a special day each year called Disaster Prevention Day. On this day, everyone pretends that an earthquake has happened.

When they are told to, people leave their homes, schools and offices and go to the nearest piece of open land. Volunteers practice putting out fires and rescuing people. The police, hospitals and fire services test out their disaster plans to see if they can cope with all the injured and lost people that will need their help.

An Earthquake Learning and **Simulation** Center has been built in Japan. The building moves just like it would if a real earthquake was happening. People who live or work in crowded city skyscrapers go to the simulation center to practice earthquake drills.

Do you have to practice earthquake drills at your school like these Japanese children?

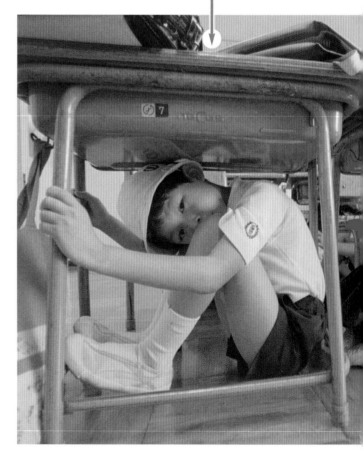

These scientists are testing a scale model of a house to see if it will stand up to the shaking of an earthquake.

Building to survive earthquakes

The best protection against earthquake damage is making sure that buildings are strong enough to withstand the shaking. Not all soils are safe to build on. Buildings need to be standing on solid rock. Those built on clay, loose sand or softer rocks will shake more and for a longer time.

By looking at the damage and the buildings that survive an earthquake, engineers can find out which building materials are the strongest and best to use. Geologists take samples of soil and rock from earthquake areas. These are tested in a laboratory to find out how the shaking of an earthquake affects them.

Hazard maps

Unfortunately, many of the world's largest cities are built on unstable ground. Earthquakes in these areas are disastrous because of the number of people living there. To help these people, engineers draw up special maps called hazard maps. A hazard map contains lots of important information about the rock layers beneath these areas. Engineers try to work out when and where earthquakes might happen in the future. They also try to guess how powerful these earthquakes might be and if they could cause other dangerous things to happen such as liquefaction, flooding or landslides. All of these things are marked on the hazard maps to help builders and town planners decide which parts of the city need to be earthquake-proofed.

Conventional building (concrete foundation): violent shaking, damage and injury

Spring building (rubber springs): gentle movement, no damage or injury

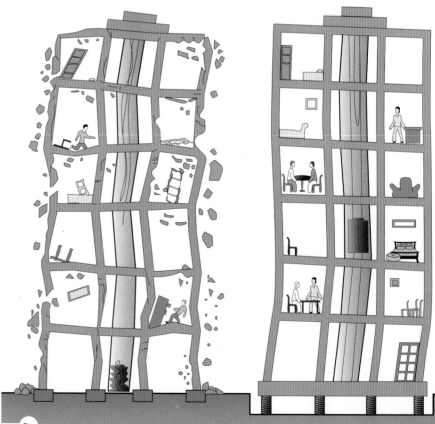

This is how new buildings are made earthquake-proof.

Mexico City is built on the soft mud of an ancient lake. In 1985, an earthquake shook the city, leaving 7,000 people dead. Tall blocks of flats collapsed because the soft mud could not support them.

This is still the scene in Armenia five years after it was struck by an earthquake. Schools and hospitals remain shut and some people live in boxes.

Earthquakes in developing countries

Earthquakes kill more people in developing countries than they do in wealthier ones. It has nothing to do with the strength of the earthquake. In developing countries there is little money available to buy strong building materials. There are not enough experts with the special equipment or knowledge needed to design and build earthquake-proof structures.

Often, the people in these countries are so poor that they have no choice but to live in very crowded and unsafe housing. In wealthier countries special laws are made to ensure that everyone is as safe as possible should an earthquake strike. When an earthquake measuring 6.9 on the Richter Scale hit San Francisco in the USA in 1989, it killed just 65 people. An earthquake of the same strength happened in the developing country of Armenia some months earlier. In 30 seconds, the earthquake killed 100,000 people and wiped out nearly all of the buildings in two of Armenia's major cities.

After an earthquake

Once the shaking has stopped, the first thing to be done is to turn off the gas and electricity to prevent fires. Rescue workers will then try to free all the people trapped in the rubble. They will use dogs that are trained to sniff out where people might be buried. They also use equipment that detects body heat, and even tiny cameras on fibers that can bend around the twisted metal and see into small, dark corners.

Hospitals are set up in tents and in buildings that have only minor damage. Community shelters with beds, hot food and bottled water are opened for the homeless who have no families to stay with. Roads have to be cleared of rubble so that help can reach the people. Boats and helicopters may be needed if bridges have fallen into rivers. As soon as it is safe to do so, the electricity supply will be reconnected. Drains and sewers will also be repaired as quickly as possible to prevent the spread of disease.

Cars can be crushed when roads crash down like this.

These people in India are searching for their families after an earthquake destroyed their homes.

When rescue workers are sure that there is nobody left inside the collapsed buildings and crushed vehicles, heavy equipment such as cranes and bulldozers will be brought in to clear away the mess. After this, rebuilding will begin. In a developed country, the city will soon be rebuilt and everybody will be back at work or school again.

What do you think might happen in developing countries? When earthquakes destroy cities in these countries, the people rely on wealthier countries to help them out with medicines, doctors, food, blankets and fresh water. You may have seen advertisements on television asking for donations of money when a disaster such as an earthquake happens.

Record-breaking earthquakes

The deadliest earthquake in history

China

A massive earthquake in the Shensi province, in 1556, killed about 830,000 people.

The deadliest earthquake in recent times

China

An earthquake measuring 7.8 on the Richter Scale hit Tangshan province on July 28, 1976. About 240,000 people died and 600,000 were seriously injured. Deaths occurred up to 200 kilometers (125 miles) from the epicenter. Nearly one million buildings collapsed.

The worst avalanche triggered by an earthquake

Peru

In 1970, an 80 meter (250 foot) wave of ice, mud and rock hurtled down the mountains in Huascarán at 400 kilometers (250 miles) an hour. It carried away entire villages and killed more than 18,000 people.

The highest tsunami caused by an earthquake

Japan

In 1771, a tsunami caused by an earthquake under the sea, which hit Ishigaki Island, was estimated to be 85 meters (278 feet) high—about the same height as a 25-story building.

The worst landslide started by an earthquake

China

A landslide killed about 200,000 people in Kansu province in 1920.

The earthquake with the most power

Chile

In 1960, an earthquake measuring 9.2 on the Richter Scale struck Chile.

Glossary

aftershocks	Tremors that follow an earthquake.
avalanche	An enormous amount of earth, snow or ice that slides down a mountainside.
continental drift	The movement of the continents across the world.
core	The center of the Earth.
crust	The hard top layer of the Earth.
debris	The remains of anything that has been broken or destroyed.
devastation	Severe damage or destruction.
earth tremor	When the Earth trembles or vibrates slightly, or a very small earthquake.
epicenter	The point on the Earth's surface where the earthquake focus is.
fault line	A break, or a weak spot, in the rocks.
focus	The place below the Earth's surface where the seismic energy is released.
fold	A bend in layers of rock.
foreshocks	Small earth movements or tremors felt before an earthquake.
geologists	Scientists who study rocks and earthquakes.
hibernation	When some animals go into a very deep sleep during the winter.
liquefaction	When soil becomes mixed with water during the shaking of an earthquake and behaves like quicksand.
magma	Hot, melted rock that is found in the Earth's mantle.
magnitude	The size or strength of an earthquake.
mantle	The layer of rock beneath the Earth's crust.
quicksand	Deep, wet sand that you sink into if you walk in it.
reservoir	A place where water is collected and stored for later use.
seismic energy	The energy released during an earthquake.
seismograph	An instrument that records and measures earth movements.
simulation	Something that is copied and made to seem real.
strainmeter	An instrument that measures the amount of strain in rocks.
tectonic plates	Plates of rock that float on top of the mantle of the Earth.
tiltmeter	An instrument used to measure the slope of the ground.
tsunami	An enormous, powerful wave that is created when an earthquake shakes the ocean floor.

Index

aftershocks 18
Aristotle 10
Armenia 14, 27
avalanche 16, 30

Chile 17, 30
China 21, 30
continental drift 8
core 6, 7
crust 6

debris 21

Earthquake Simulation Center
    24
engineers 25, 26
epicenter 14

fault line 10, 12
fire 18
floods 17
focus 14
fold 9
foreshocks 21

geologists 19, 21–23, 25
Great Kanto earthquake 18

hazard maps 26
Himalayas 9

Japan 15, 18, 24, 30

landslides 16, 30
laser beams 22
liquefaction 16

magma 6, 10
magnitude 20
mantle 6
Mercalli Scale 20
Mexico City 27

New Zealand 12, 17

P waves 13

Richter Scale 19, 20

S waves 13
San Andreas Fault 10, 22
satellites 23
seismic energy 13
seismograph 19
strainmeter 23
surface waves 13

tectonic plates 8, 11
tiltmeter 23
tsunami 17, 30

Zhang Heng 19